Mazes
For Kids Ages 8-12

This book belongs to:

_____

Thank you for choosing our maze book. It's great that you like mazes books as much as we do! These activities offer hours of fun and are a great way to improve your focus and concentration.

There are all kinds of mazes activities. In this book, we've organized it from easy to hard difficulty levels!

Once you complete the book, there will be a certificate of completion waiting for you as your reward.

Have fun and enjoy!

Level 1

Let's start! In this level, you will go through easy mazes.

Ready? Let's go!

CAT FOOD

MAGIC

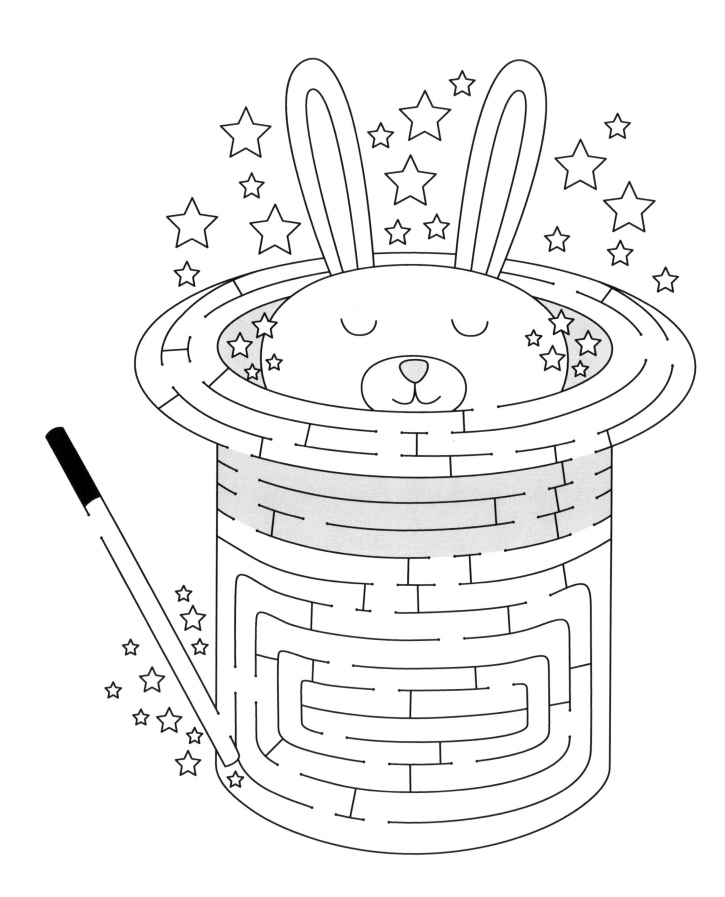

NUT

HAT

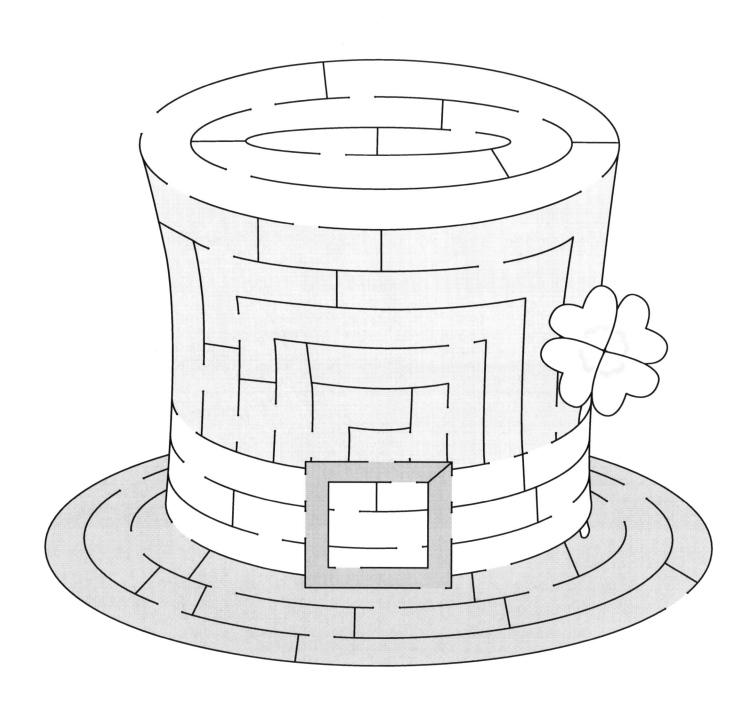

GIFTS

EXPLORE

PEPPA PIG

LEMONADE

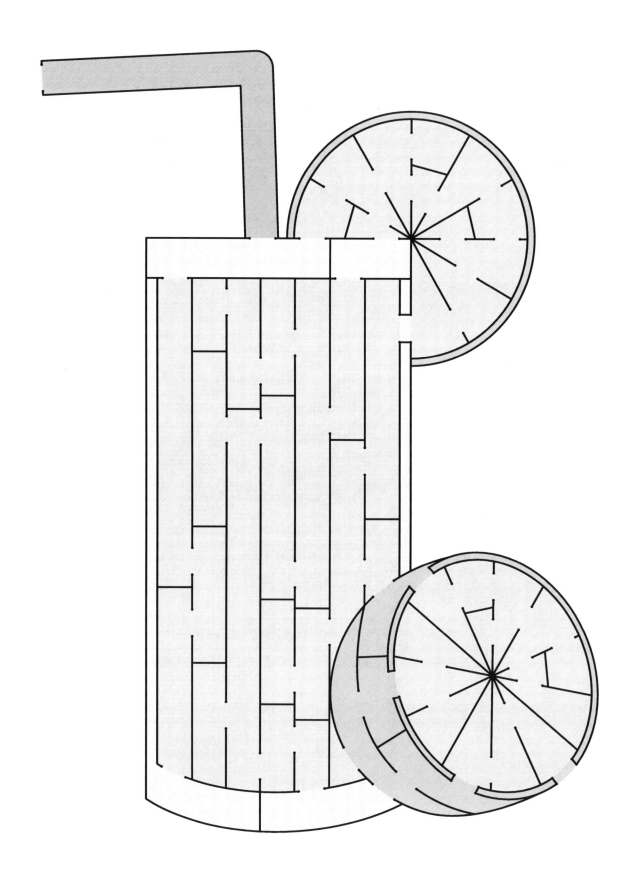

PANDA

CHRISTMAS

STARS

SPIDER

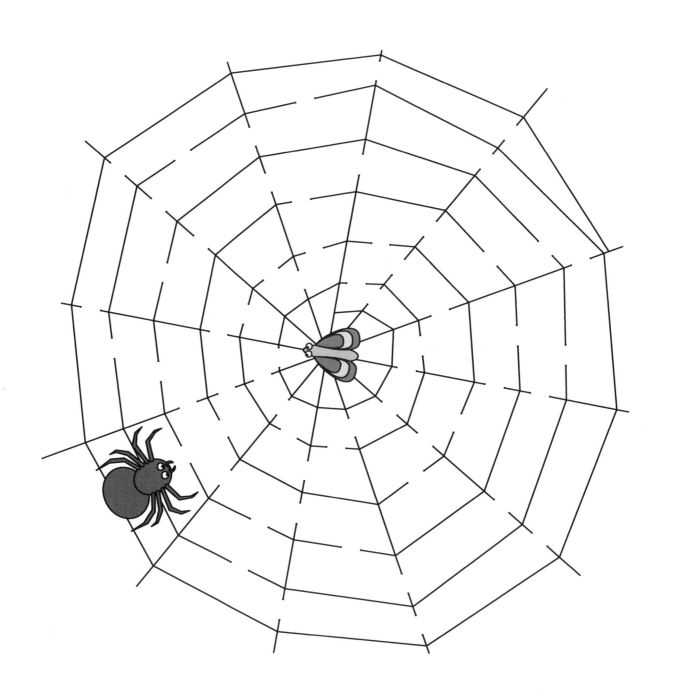

SHELL

HAPPY BIRTHDAY

PONY

BOOK

SPACE

BUNNY

COFFEE

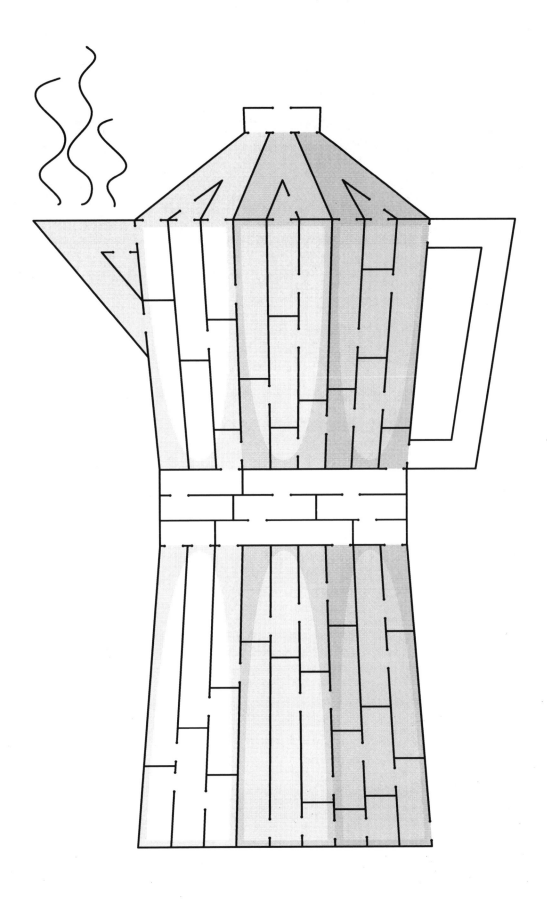

DOCTOR

FLOWER

PLANETS

LOVE

BUTTERFLY

MOON

FROG

Level 2

In this level, you will go through medium difficulty mazes.

Ready? Let's go!

SAY CHEESE

PIZZA

HALLOWEEN

PINEAPPLE

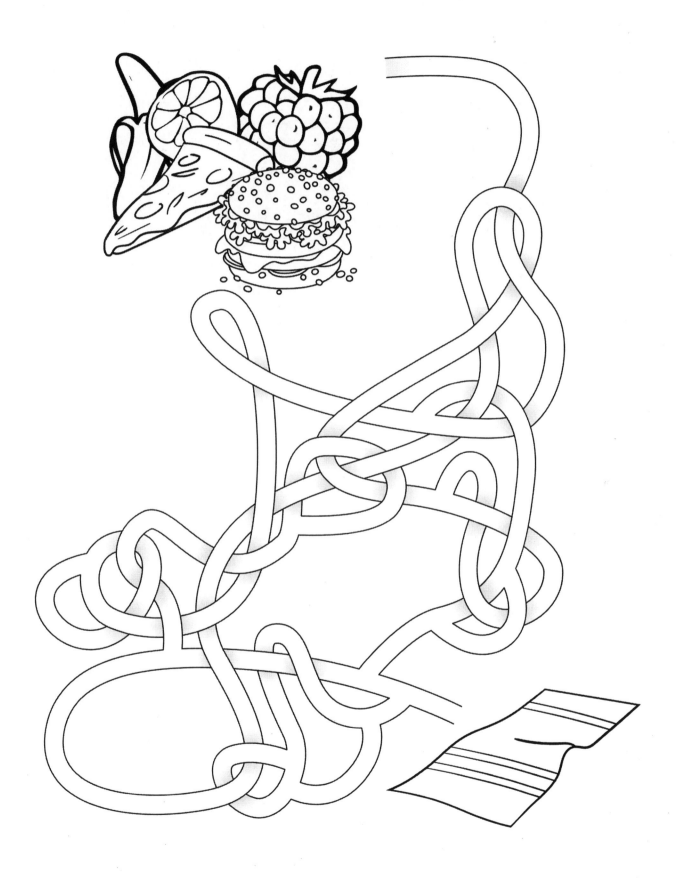

CORN

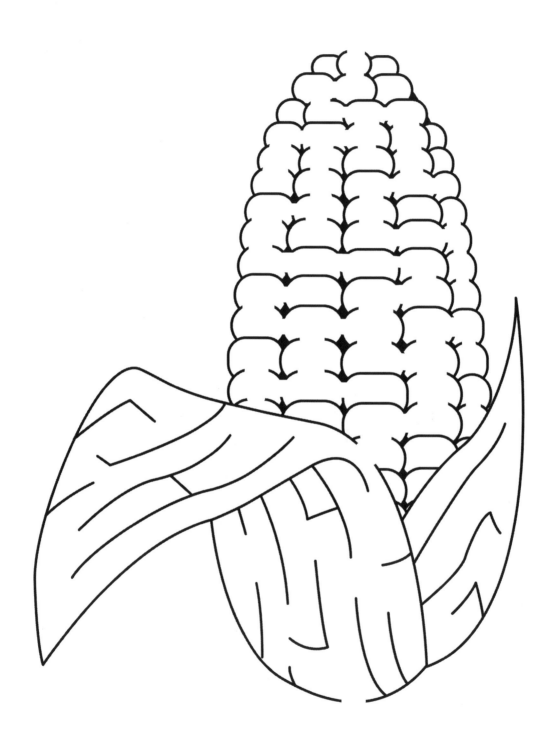

DOG

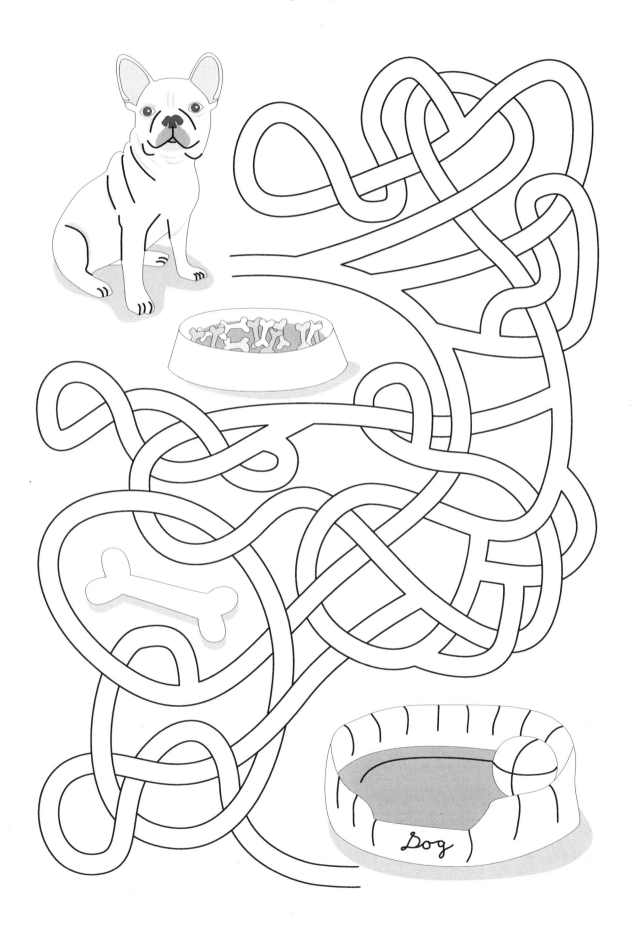

TREASURE

PIE

LETTER

HOUSE

SEAHORSE

SUNDAY TREAT

APPLE PICKING

ELEPHANTS

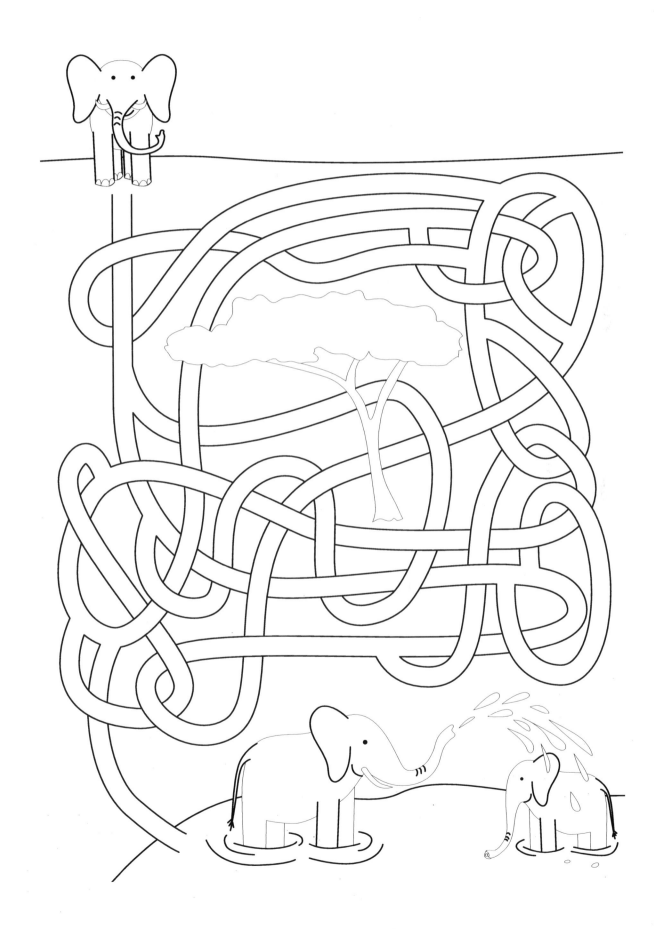

DINOSAUR

DOLPHIN

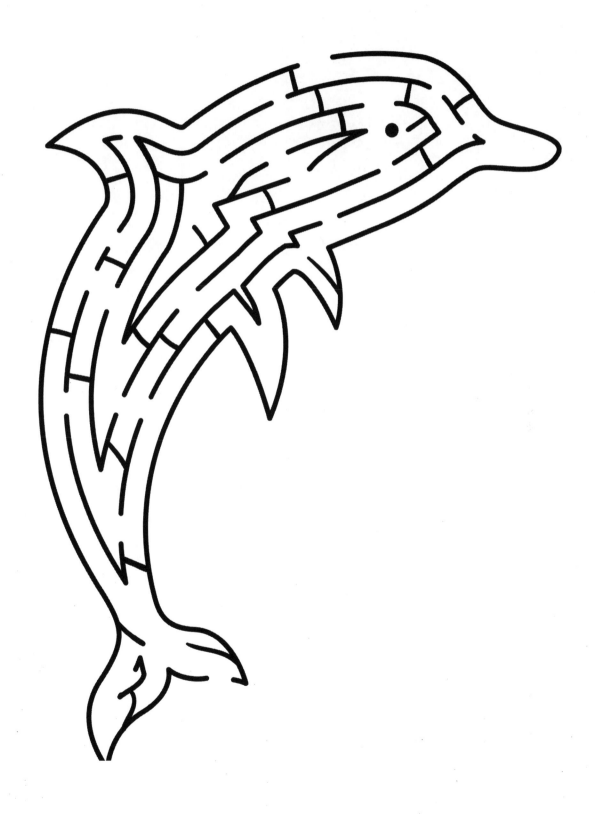

HORSE

PAINT PALETTE

FLAG

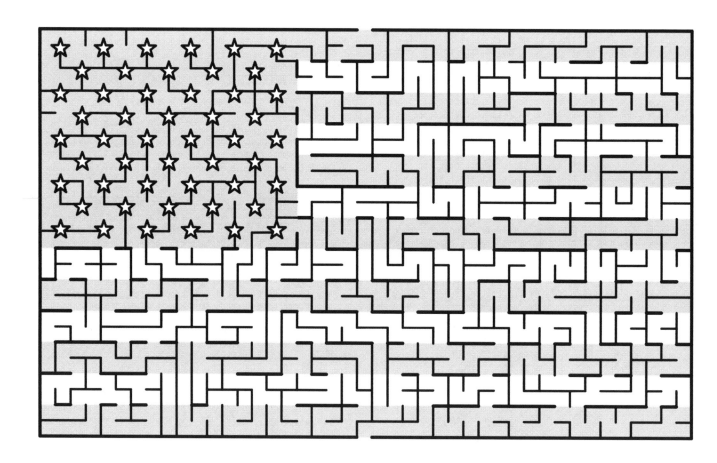

GLOBE

WATER PARK

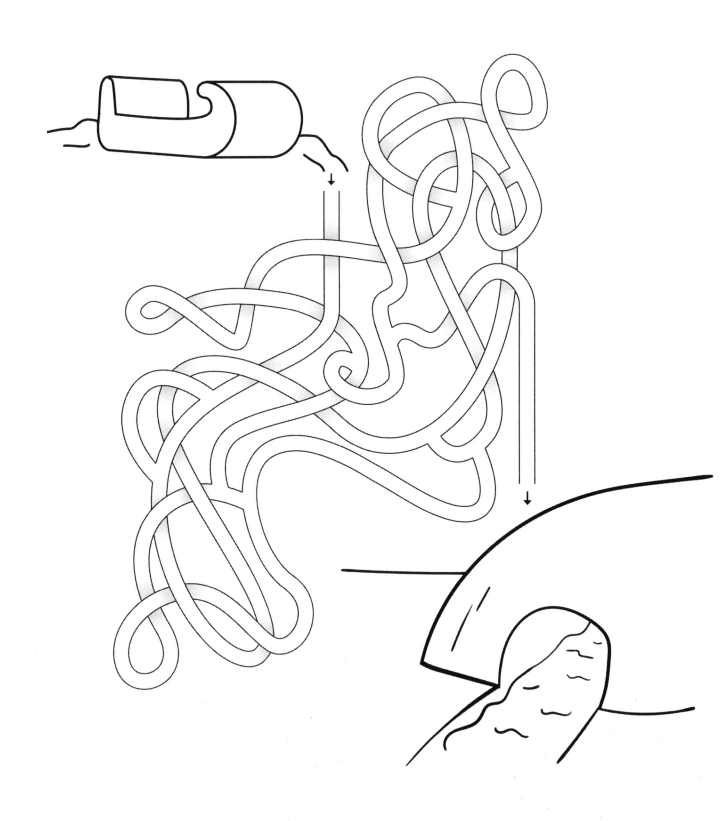

NORTH POLE

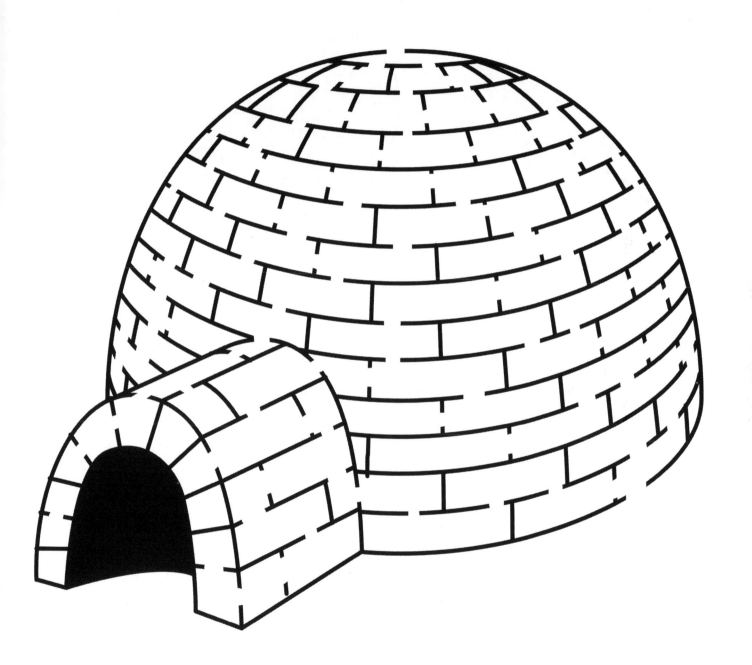

MR. TURTLE

FAMILY BOAT

PINEAPPLE

SNAIL

YOGA

Level 3

Wow you made it far!

In this level, you will go through more difficult mazes.

Ready? Let's go!

PEACOCKS

JUICE BOX

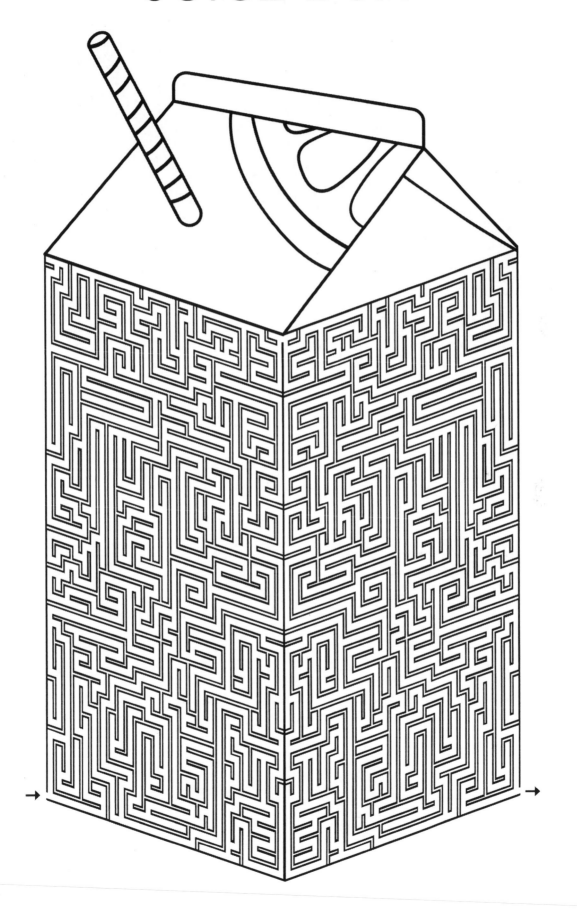

THE AWESOME
BIRTHDAY CAKE

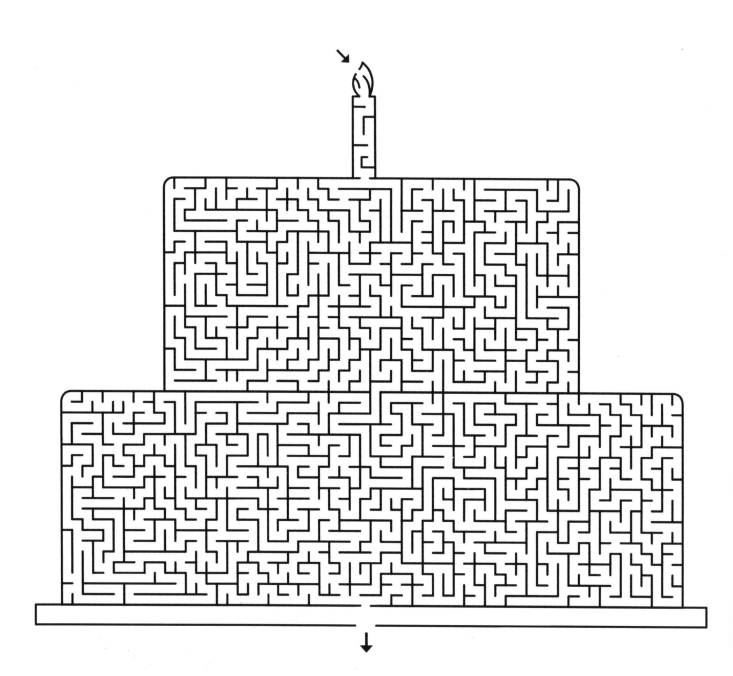

HELICOPTER

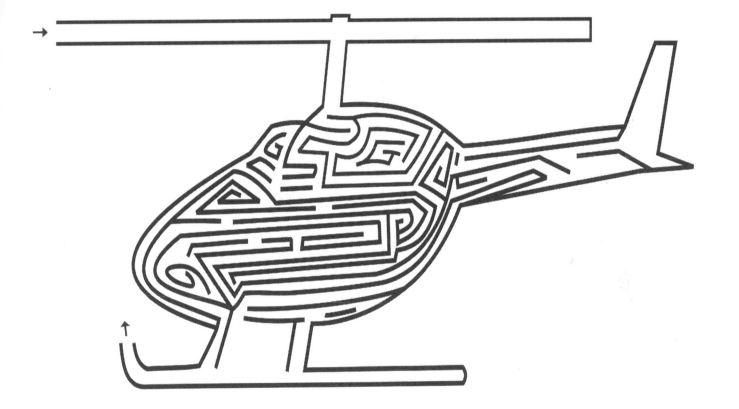

SPIDER WEB

TEDDY BEAR

LAPTOP

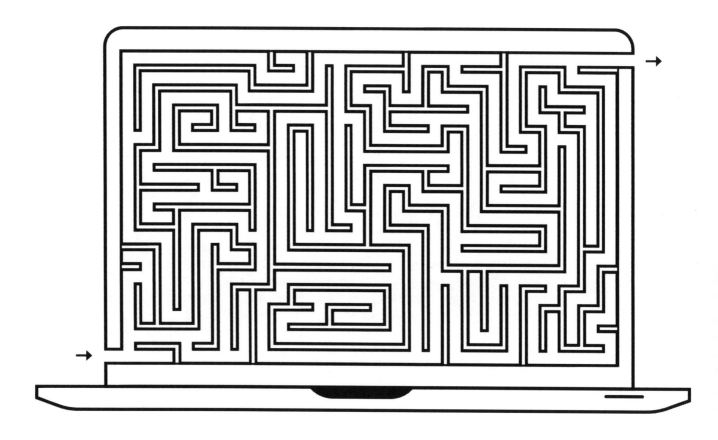

ROCKETSHIP

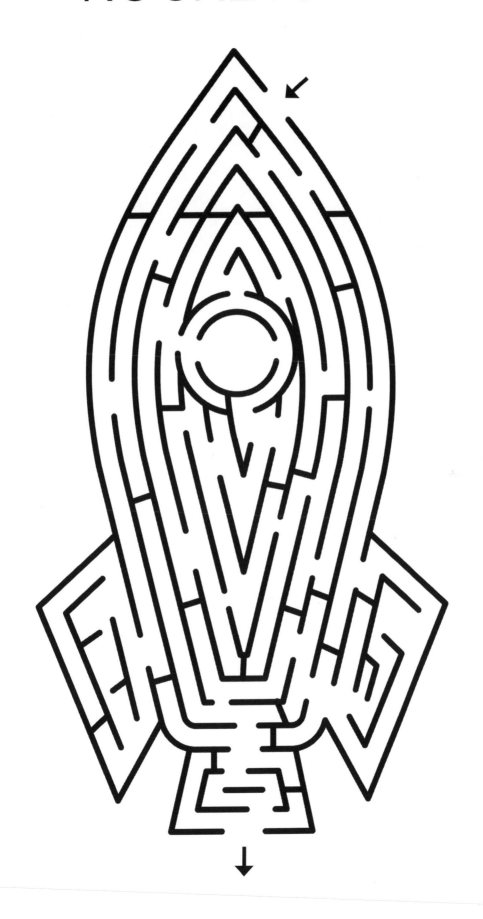

SAND TOYS

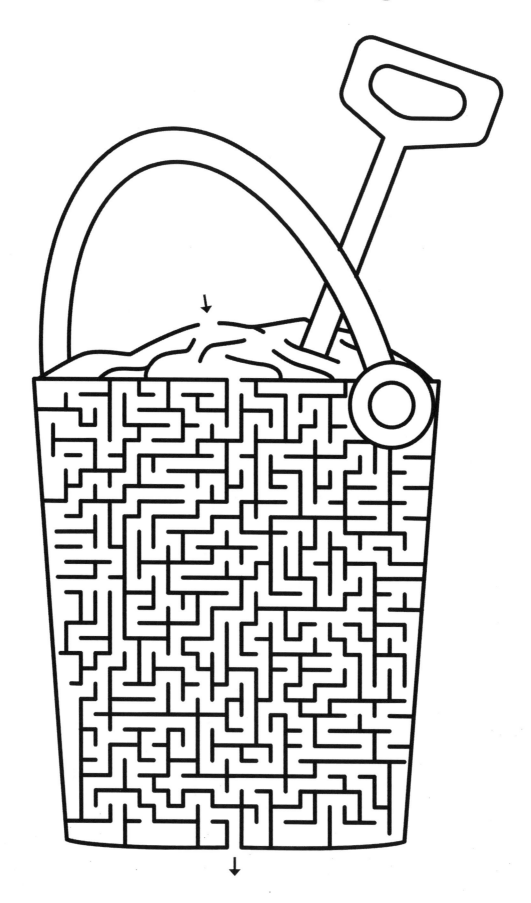

MOVIE SNACKS

FRIENDSHIP
BRACELET

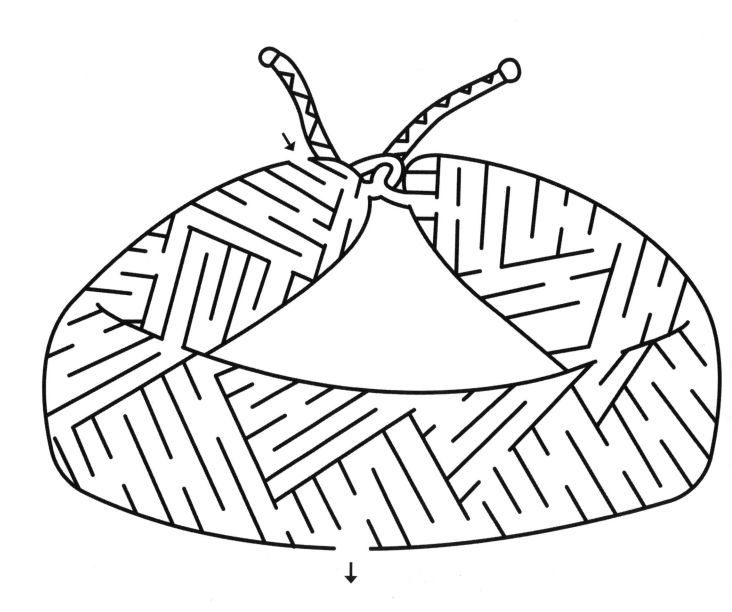

BATHTIME

SOCCER BALL

RAIN DROP

KANGAROO

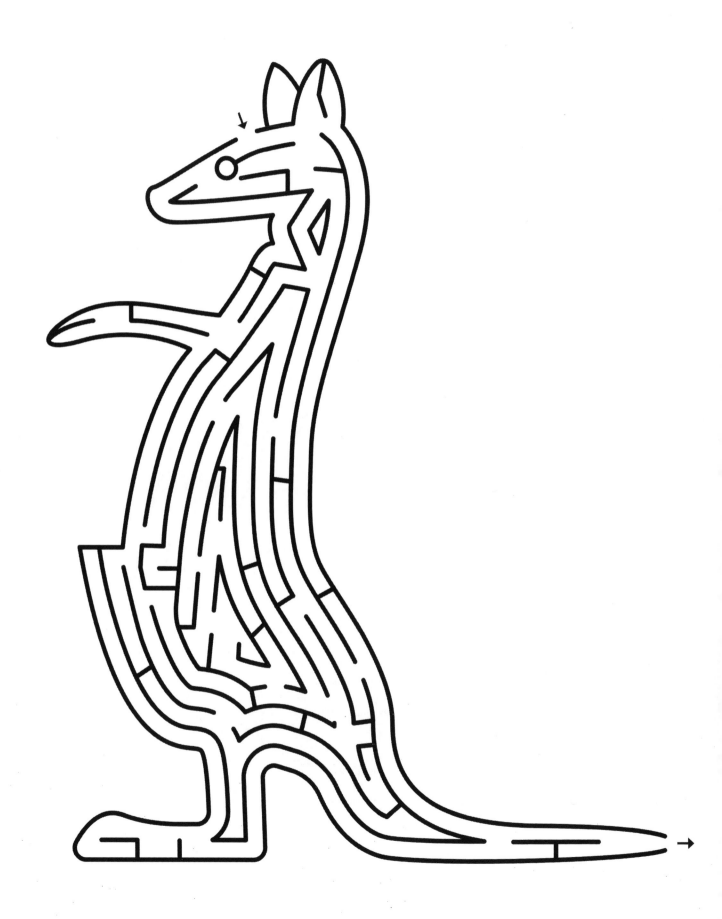

BUS TRIP

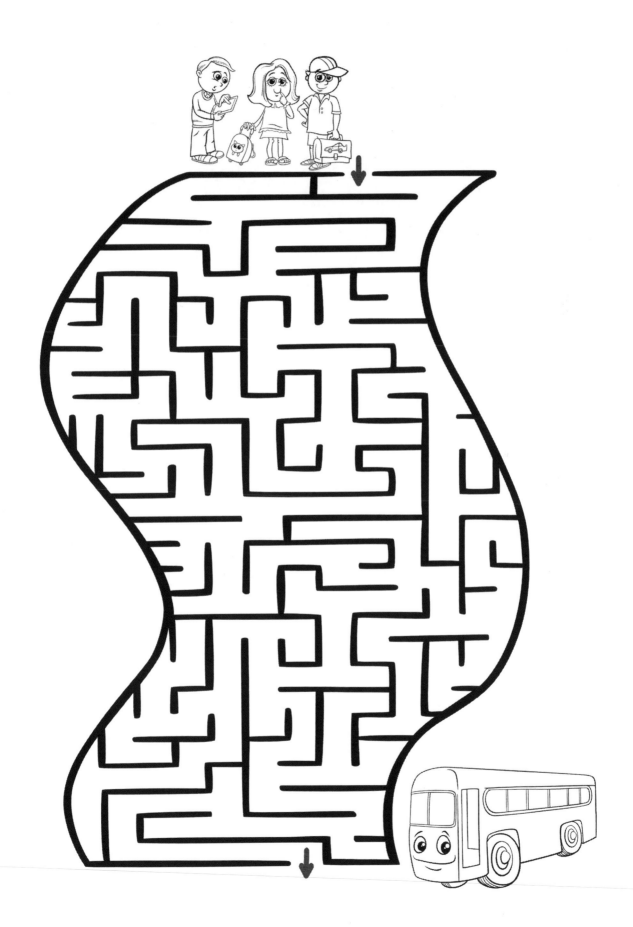

DAILY CHORES

STRAWBERRY JAM

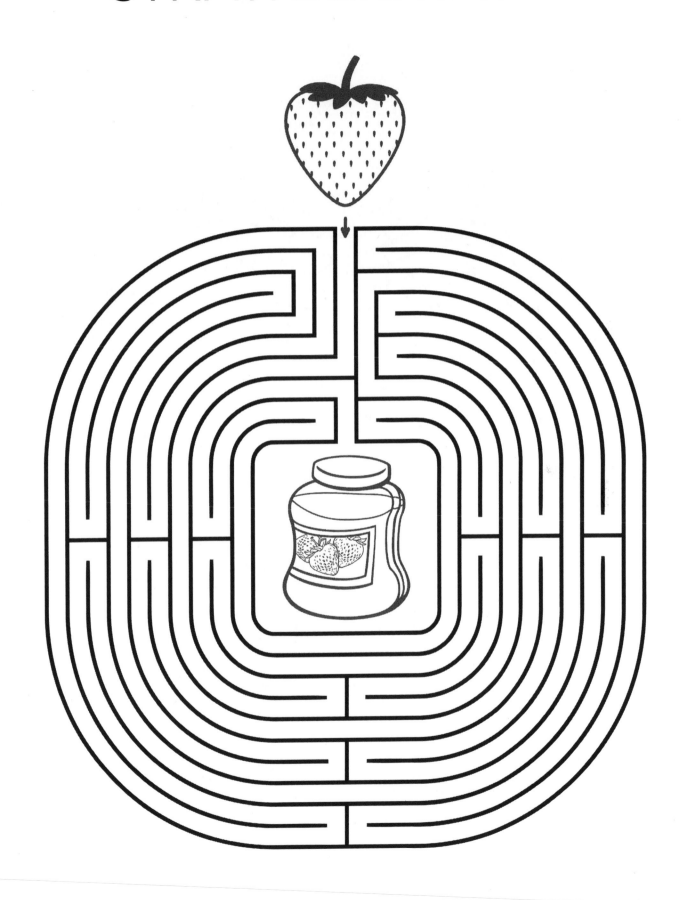

MY COOL T-SHIRT

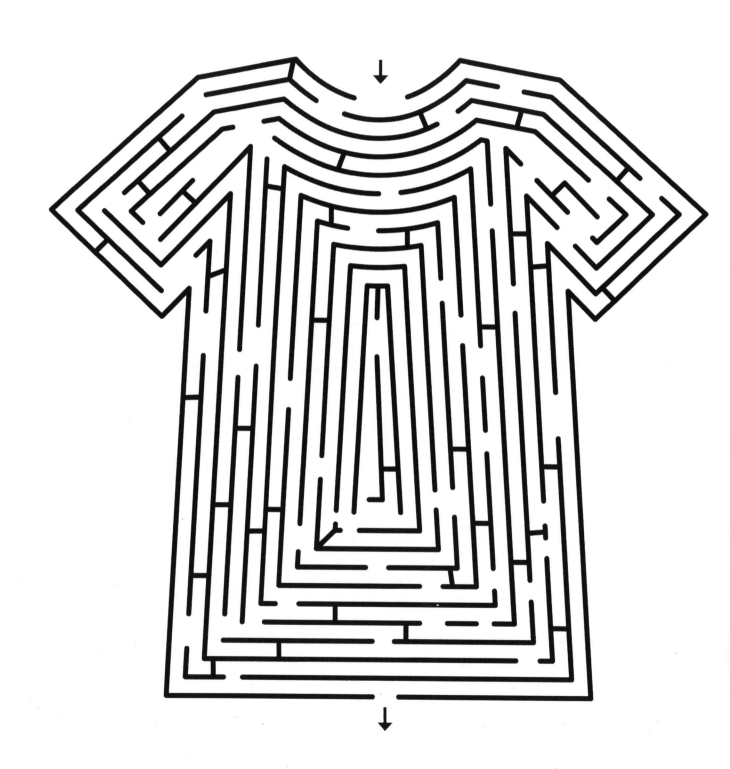

HANGER

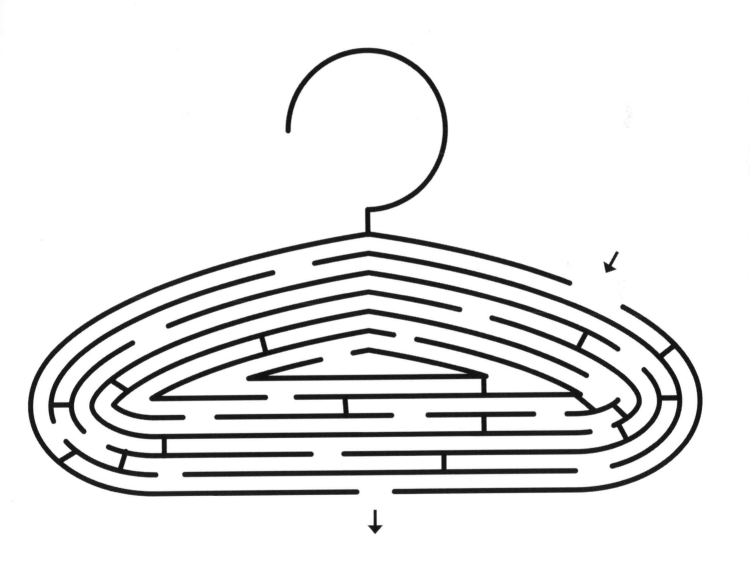

PIZZA SLICE

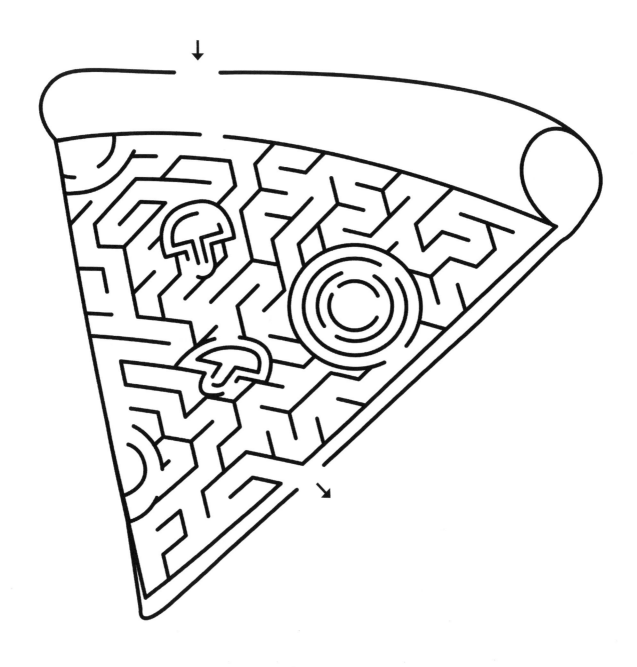

MY WALLET

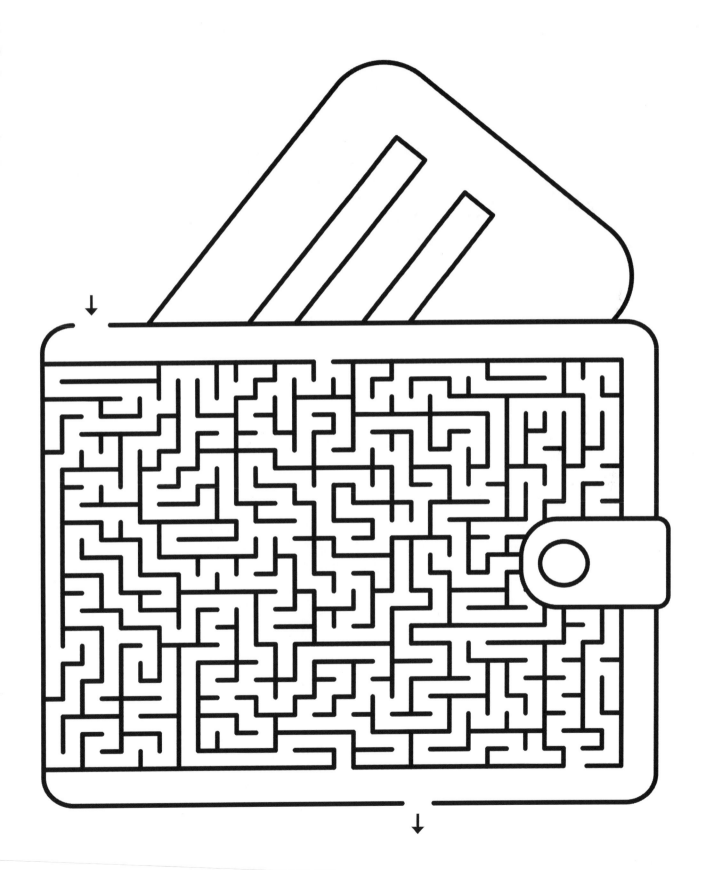

RACE TRACK

VALENTINES

TUCAN

THE ZOO

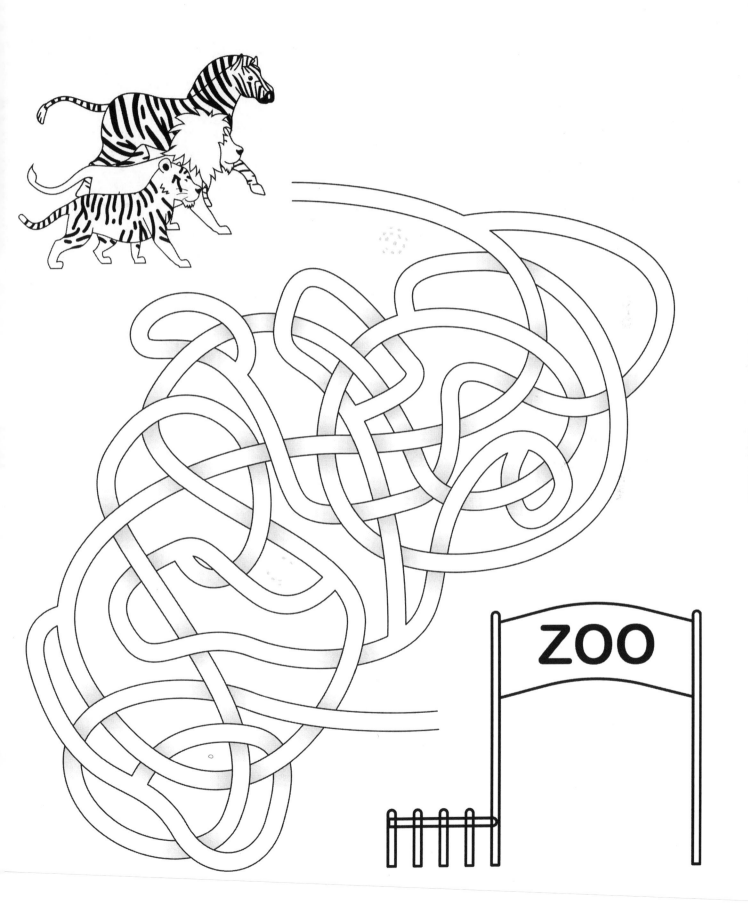

ORIGAMI

CONGRATULATIONS!

You're truly amazing! I am sure there are some obstacles along the way; it was great you persisted through and finished the job!

If you want to continue with some more word searches, just send me an email to hello.jennifer.trace@gmail.com and I will send you some printable word searches for free.

My name is Jennifer Trace and I hope you found this workbook helpful and fun. If you have any suggestions about how to improve this book, changes to make or how to make it more useful, please let me know.

If you like this book, would you be so kind and leave me a review on Amazon.

Thank you very much!
Jennifer Trace

Congratulations
Mazes Star:

THE BEST!

_____

Date:_____   Signed:_____

3. CAT FOOD

4. MAGIC

5. NUT
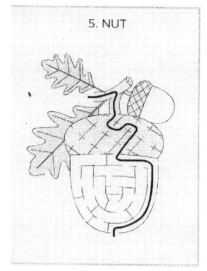

6. HAT
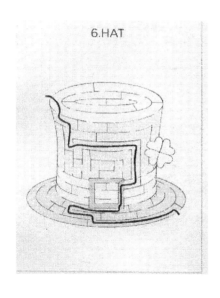

7. GIFTS

8. EXPLORE

9. PEPPA PIG

10. LEMONADE
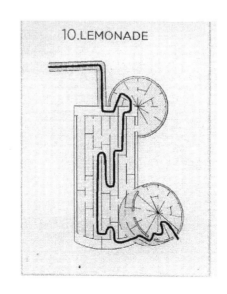

11. PANDA
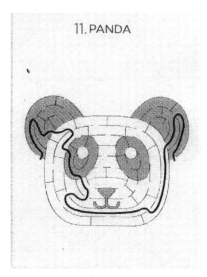

ANSWER KEY

12.CHRISTMAS

13.STARS
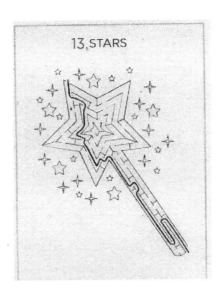

14.SPIDER
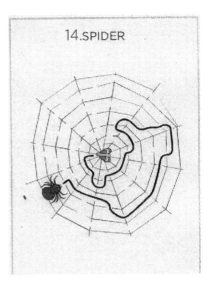

15.SHELL

16.HAPPY BIRTHDAY
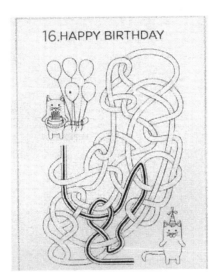

17.PONY

18.BOOK

19.SPACE
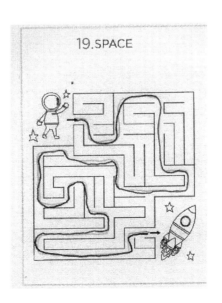

20.BUNNY
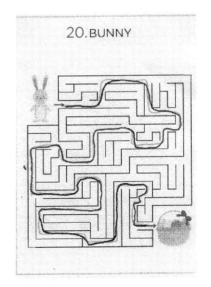

LEVEL 1

ANSWER KEY

21. COFFEE
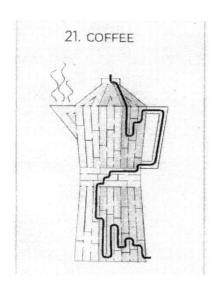

22. DOCTOR
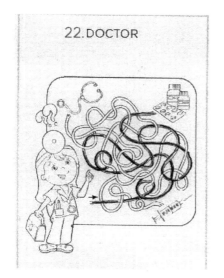

23. FLOWERS

24. PLANETS
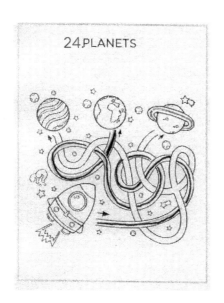

25. LOVE

26. BUTTERFLY
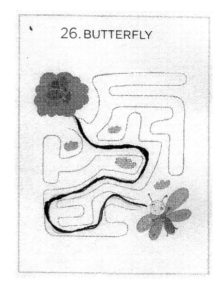

27. MOON

28. FROG

LEVEL 1

30. SAY CHEESE

31. PIZZA
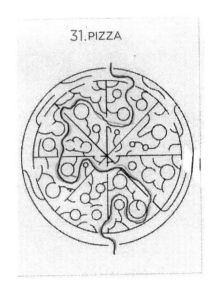

32. HALLOWEEN

33. PINEAPPLE
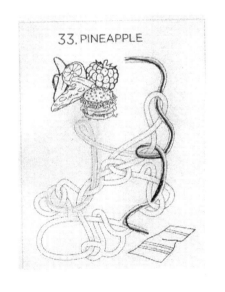

34. CORN
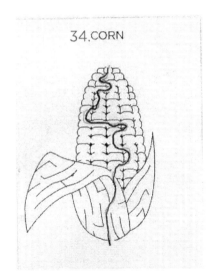

35. DOG

36. TREASURE

37. PIE

38. LETTER

39. HOUSE

39. HOUSE

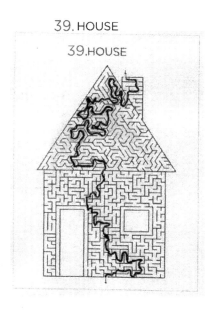

40. SEAHORSE

41. SUNDAY TREAT

42. APPLE PICKING

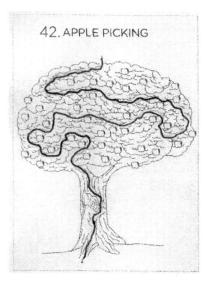

43. ELEPHANTS

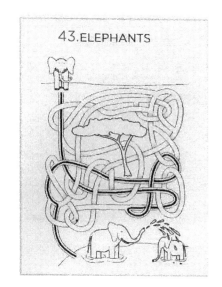

44. DINOSAUR

45. DOLPHIN

46. HORSE

47. PAINT PALETTE

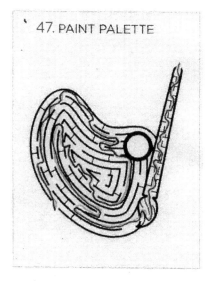

48. FLAG
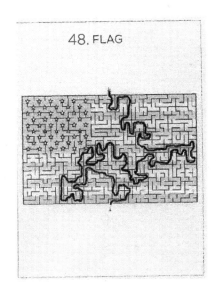

49. GLOBE
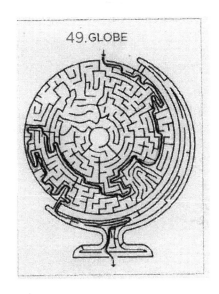

50. WATER PARK
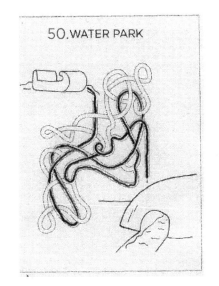

51. NORTH POLE
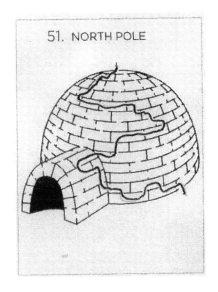

52. MR. TURTLE
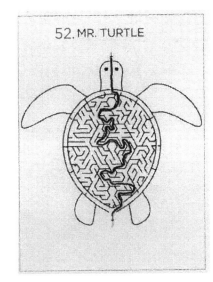

53. FAMILY BOAT
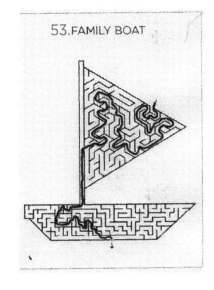

54. PINEAPPLE

55. SNAIL
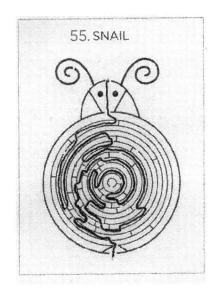

56. YOGA

58. PEACOCKS

59. JUICE BOX

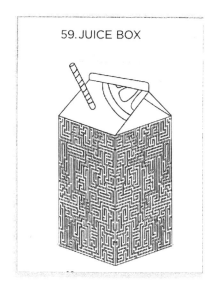

60. THE AWESOME BIRTHDAY CAKE

61. HELICOPTER

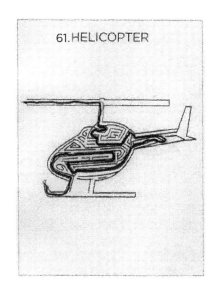

62. SPIDER WEB

63. TEDDY BEAR

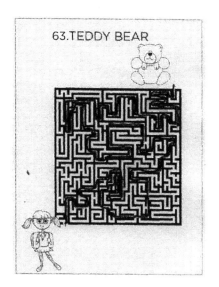

64. LAPTOP

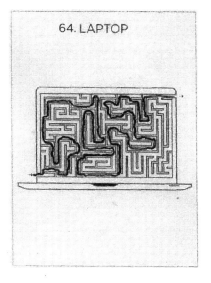

65. ROCKETSHIP

66. SAND TOYS

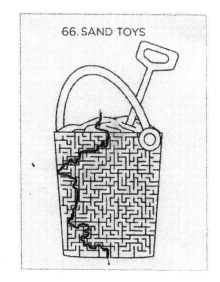

67. MOVIE SNACKS
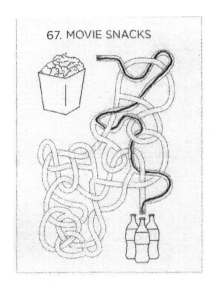

68. FRIENDSHIP BRACELET
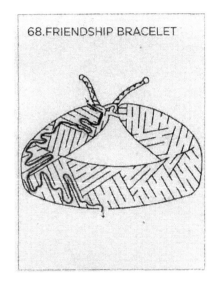

69. BATHTIME
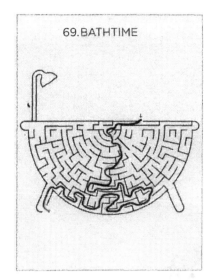

70. SOCCER BALL

71. RAIN DROP
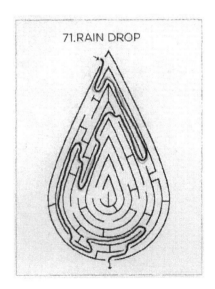

72. KANGAROO
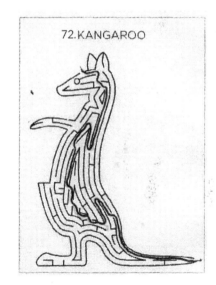

73. BUS TRIP
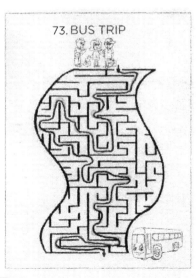

74. DAILY CHORES

75. STRAWBERRY JAM
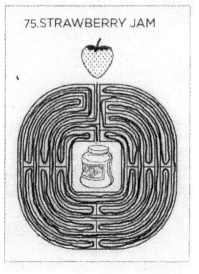

76. MY COOL T-SHIRT

77. HANGER
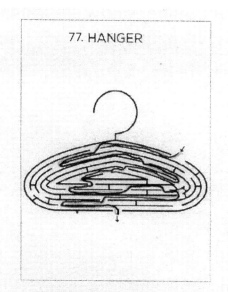

78. PIZZA SLICE
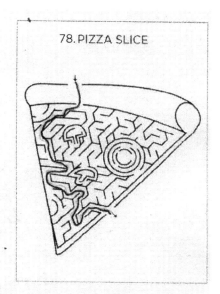

79. MY WALLET
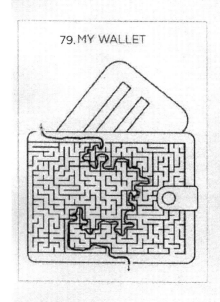

80. RACE TRACK
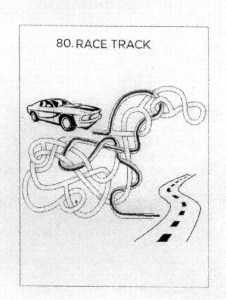

81. VALENTINES

82. TUCAN

83. THE ZOO

84. ORIGAMI
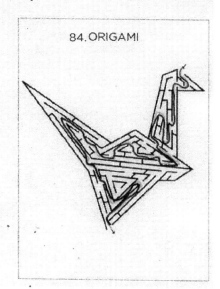

Made in the USA
Las Vegas, NV
28 November 2021